HAL•LEONARD
INSTRUMENTAL PLAY-ALONG

AUDIO ACCESS INCLUDED

PLAYBACK+
Speed • Pitch • Balance • Loop

FLUTE

Disney
Beauty AND THE Beast

D0504008

ISBN 978-1-4950-9609-9

Motion Picture Artwork, TM & Copyright
© 2017 Disney Enterprises, Inc.

Wonderland Music Company, Inc.
Walt Disney Music Company

DISTRIBUTED BY

HAL•LEONARD®

7777 W. BLUEMOUND RD. P.O. BOX 13819 MILWAUKEE, WI 53213

In Australia Contact:
Hal Leonard Australia Pty. Ltd.
4 Lentara Court
Cheltenham, Victoria, 3192 Australia
Email: ausadmin@halleonard.com.au

Visit Hal Leonard Online at
www.halleonard.com

4

ARIA

FLUTE

Music by ALAN MENKEN
Lyrics by TIM RICE

Moderately, getting faster throughout

Harpsichord

BE OUR GUEST

Flute

Music by ALAN MENKEN
Lyrics by HOWARD ASHMAN

BEAUTY AND THE BEAST

FLUTE

Music by ALAN MENKEN
Lyrics by HOWARD ASHMAN

BELLE

FLUTE

Music by ALAN MENKEN
Lyrics by HOWARD ASHMAN

DAYS IN THE SUN

FLUTE

Music by ALAN MENKEN
Lyrics by TIM RICE

EVERMORE

FLUTE

Music by ALAN MENKEN
Lyrics by TIM RICE

GASTON

FLUTE

Music by ALAN MENKEN
Lyrics by HOWARD ASHMAN

HOW DOES A MOMENT LAST FOREVER

FLUTE

Music by ALAN MENKEN
Lyrics by TIM RICE

THE MOB SONG

Flute

Music by ALAN MENKEN
Lyrics by HOWARD ASHMAN

SOMETHING THERE

FLUTE

Music by ALAN MENKEN
Lyrics by HOWARD ASHMAN